HELP!
I've Been Called By God

Easy Steps to Preparing and Delivering a Message

TARSHA L. CAMPBELL

Copyright © 2004, 2007 by Tarsha L. Campbell
ISBN-13: 978-0-9755234-0-7
ISBN-10: 0-9755234-0-6
First Printing 2004
Second Printing 2007, revised
Third Printing 2008, revised
Fourth Printing 2010, revised

All Rights Reserved. No part of this book may be reproduced or transmitted in any form or by any means, electronically or mechanically, including photocopying, recording or by an information storage and retrieval system without permission in writing from the author of this book.

Unless otherwise indicated, all scripture quotations are taken from the King James Version of the Holy Bible.

Verses marked Amplified Bible are taken from the Amplified Bible, Copyright © 1954, 1958, 1962, 1964, 1965, 1987 by The Lockman Foundation. Used by permission.

Scripture quotations marked (NIV) are taken from the HOLY BIBLE, NEW INTERNATIONAL VERSION®. NIV®. Copyright© 1973, 1978, 1984 by International Bible Society. Used by permission of Zondervan. All rights reserved.

Cover & Interior Design by Tarsha L. Campbell
Edited by Donna L. Ferrier
Proofread by Sharlyne Thomas and Ayana Campbell

Published by:
DOMINIONHOUSE
Publishing & Design
P.O. Box 681938 | Orlando, Florida 32868 | 407.880.5790
www.mydominionhouse.com
The Lord gave the word: great was the company of those that published it. (Psalms 68:11)

DEDICATION

*This book is dedicated to every servant
of the most high God
who desires to do the will of the Father.
May you abound in the things
to which you have been called.*

ACKNOWLEDGEMENT

To my Loving Father God, thank you for entrusting me with such great and precious promises. I want to thank you for blessing me with my coat of many colors, which I wear humbly before you and your people. To my loving Lord and Savior, I thank you for your sacrifice of love. Without your gift of redemption I wouldn't have access to the Father's treasures. I owe you my life. To the precious Holy Spirit, my friend and trusted companion. We both know the truth... I couldn't do what I do without you. Thank you...I need you.

Special thanks to my wonderful husband Dwayne, you know you're my hero. You can save me any day. To my beautiful children, Ayana & Dakarai, thanks for allowing me to take time to complete this project. I am proud of you. You're the best! To my mother, Dr. Pastor Betty Jamison, and my spiritual mother, Pastor Alma Perry, your prayers, intercession and friendship are more valuable than gold. To my granny, Everlina Dixon, and my aunt, Sarah Davis, thank you for keeping watch with your prayers and intercession. To Pastor Bernice Rahming, my new spiritual mom, thanks for your encouraging words, prayers and seeing the gifts within me.

To my all my spiritual sisters during this season in my life (too many to name...you know who you are). Thanks for having my back in the spirit. I feel your prayers & intercession. Go forth and conquer new territory! I got your back.

This acknowledgement would not be complete if I didn't express my gratitude to my former pastor and church family, the late Apostle Curtis Lake Jr. and Deliverance Miracle Revival Center, Inc. For it was my years of service under his tutorage and covering which has afforded me this opportunity to write about ministry. For that I am grateful.

TABLE OF CONTENTS

Introduction

Chapter 1: Preparing a Message 11
- Choose a Subject for Your Message/Sermon
- Find a Scripture Reference Text
- Find at Least Two Biblical Examples to Support Your Subject
- Find Up-to-Date Examples to Support the Subject
- Develop Your Conclusion for the Message/Sermon
- Practice Message

Chapter 2: Delivering the Message 21
- Do All of Your Preliminaries First
- State Your Subject
- Give Your Scripture Reference Text
- Explain the Text
- Discuss Your Biblical Examples
- Bring it Up to Date
- Recap Your Points and Conclude the Message
- End With a Prayer

Chapter 3: Fasting and Prayer:
Keys to Ministry 31
- Fasting and Prayer
- Different Types of Prayer
- The Complete Fast
- Keys to Remember When Fasting

Chapter 4: How to Study God's Word 47
- Choose a Subject and Research it Thoroughly
- Attend Bible Studies, Church Services, Conferences and Seminars
- Expose Yourself to God's Word Constantly
- Study Regularly and Seek God for Understanding

Chapter 5: Wisdom in Ministry 53
- The Importance of Wisdom in Ministry
- Wisdom Keys for Ministry

Chapter 6: The Five-Fold Ministry 59
- Apostles
- Prophets
- Evangelists
- Pastors
- Teachers

About the Author 66

INTRODUCTION

This book addresses the importance of preparing and delivering a message (or sermon) and provides steps to accomplishing this goal. This text not only deals with the process of actually preparing the message, but also with the preparation of the spirit and heart on the part of the speaker before he or she ever sets pen to paper.

I wanted to present this guide for two reasons. First of all, I know that God is calling yielded vessels to speak a Word for Him like never before. And while these messengers (and you may be one of them) have a call and Word from the Lord, many of these individuals have not had the opportunity to receive any type of formal seminary training. This easy and simple guide, therefore, is designed for such individuals who need help preparing and delivering a message.

Secondly, I've observed ministers on several occasions who preach and teach without a specific format. Using this method, however, often leaves listeners confused and dismayed because the message was too fragmented to understand and apply in their own lives. Ministers who have sermons with no format tend to jump from subject to subject, hitting a point here and there; and unfortunately, never accomplishing the intended goal, which is to edify the listener (meaning to instruct or enlighten). As ministers of the Gospel, our job is to make sure our audience clearly hears what God has to say.

I encourage you, as God opens doors for you to minister, to use this guide to help you confidently deliver His Word with skill and maximum effectiveness.

Chapter 1
Preparing a Message

This chapter contains a standard format for preparing a message, complete with step-by-step instructions for its use, that can be used each time you speak. As you grow and mature in your delivery, the format can be modified to suit your own personal style as the Spirit leads. The format is as follows:

1. Choose a Subject for Your Message/Sermon

When choosing a subject for your message/sermon, it's important to pray and be led by the Spirit. He knows what your audience needs to hear, the impact He wants to make, and you can't go wrong following His lead. Let's say the Spirit gives you the subject, "Warriors for God." Now you have a starting point. On to Step 2.

2. Find a Scripture Reference Text

Finding a scripture reference text basically means finding scriptures that best support the subject of your message. This is very important because the scripture reference text serves as a spiritual footprint that leaves an indelible impression upon listeners' hearts from the Word of God. Also, showing that your message is based on the Word adds validity to your sermon. If God has not revealed a specific scripture He wants you to use, find a concordance and look up some of the main words in your subject.

The scripture reference text doesn't need to be long (like an entire chapter); in fact, it's best not to present a long scripture reference text unless the Spirit has led you to do so. Hearers tend to get lost in long text passages, and you may have to work to regain their attention. For more expository preaching, (i.e., if the Spirit leads you to pull insights from a passage line upon line) using a larger scripture passage is okay. Beginners, however, should keep it simple.

For our practice message/sermon, "Warriors for God," we would most likely look up the word "warriors", or words related to war. You may have a concordance in the back of your Bible, but for a complete exhaustive concordance, I suggest, *The New Strong's Exhaustive Concordance of the Bible*, published by Nelson Publishers. This concordance offers a variety of aids, such as scripture reference text entries and the original Hebrew or Greek meanings of words. For our sample message, you might discover 1 Timothy 6.12 in your concordance which says, "Fight the good fight of faith…."

Once you have your scripture reference text, you can study other words found in the text and cross reference other scriptures that could be used to support your message throughout your delivery. Studying the scripture reference text in this manner can also help you break down key words and find definitions to use throughout your message.

When I prepare a message, I like to use a) the Hebrew or Greek meanings to create a foundation on which the message will stand, and b) definitions from key words in the scripture reference text to help my hearers understand the subject more clearly. I find as I meditate upon my key scriptures, definitions, and Hebrew or Greek meanings, the Spirit begins to speak more deeply. So I encourage you to use this time to really hear a) what the Spirit wants to say to you personally, and b) what He wants to say to the people He is sending you to. The Word of the Lord comes to speak to the messenger's life first and his or her audience second. Now let's move on to Step 3.

3. Find at Least Two Biblical Examples to Support Your Subject

Step 3 is when your message really begins to take shape. Your biblical examples serve as support beams for your entire message/sermon. Using biblical examples will help you build your case and serve as a witness to the truth. According to Hebrews 12:1 in the Amplified Bible, biblical examples are called "a great cloud of witnesses":

> THEREFORE THEN, since we are surrounded by so great a cloud of witnesses [who have borne testimony to the Truth], let us strip off and throw aside every encumbrance (unnecessary weight) and that sin which so readily (deftly and cleverly) clings to and entangles us, and let us run with patient

endurance and steady and active persistence the appointed course of the race that is set before us.

Biblical examples of men and women whose experiences can help us learn and grow will help your listeners identify with the subject of your message, which in this case, is "Warriors for God." For this subject, let's use Samson's battle with the Philistines as well as David's battle with Goliath. Both stories depict warriors for God at work. In the next chapter, "Delivering the Message," I will discuss how to use these biblical examples in your message/sermon; but for now, let us move on to Step 4.

4. Find Up-to-Date Examples to Support the Subject

This step helps your listeners relate to the subject of your message further and helps you drive key points home. Using up-to-date examples pulls the hearers in and inspires, awakens and challenges them to greater truth. Your examples do not have to be biblical or church related to be effective. Depending on the subject of your message, you may be able to use your own wisely presented life experiences. People tend to connect with the message when they see that the minister understands the subject on a personal level. For our sample message, we might use the warriors of Desert Storm as an up-to-date example. Now let us move on to Step 5.

5. Develop Your Conclusion for the Message/Sermon

At this point, simply recap what you've said. Reinforce your points, and make your closing statements. Many ministers go astray at this point because they don't have a conclusion to their message; therefore, they start talking about something totally unrelated to their subject. Having a planned conclusion prevents this from happening. When developing your conclusion, concentrate on the state of mind you want to leave your listeners in. Specific methods for developing your conclusion will be discussed in the next chapter, "Delivering the Message."

Rest assured, the format provided in this chapter has been tested and tried many times over, and found to be effective. So the next time you minister, try this simple format for preparing a message.

Practice Message

Use the outline provided below to prepare a message/sermon

(You will find more practice outlines in the back of the book)

I. Message/Sermon Subject

    A. _____

    _____

II. Scripture Reference Text(s)

    A. _____

    B. _____

III. Two Biblical Examples to Support My Subject

    A. _____

    B. _____

IV. Up-to-Date Examples to Support My Subject

    A. _____

    B. _____

    C. _____

V. Message/Sermon Conclusion

    A. Reinforce/reiterate my points

_____

_____

_____

_____

_____

_____

    B. Closing Statements/Prayer

_____

_____

_____

_____

_____

_____

_____

_____

_____

_____

_____

_____

Chapter 2
DELIVERING THE MESSAGE

In Chapter 1 we discussed preparing a message. Here we will discuss delivering the message. A perfectly prepared message doesn't do any good if it's not delivered effectively. 1 Corinthians 14:40 says, "Let all things be done decently and in order." A poorly delivered message only tends to confuse the listeners, causing them to miss what God is trying to say. Let's start from the beginning.

1. Do All of Your Preliminaries First

The first step is to be sure to recognize overseers, pastors and other ministers or leaders present in your audience. Be wise; do this in a manner that doesn't offend anyone. A simple statement such as, "I give honor to all God's men and women in the service today," should suffice. If you're a guest minister at another church, also acknowledge your own church's leaders and congregation. And remember to acknowledge the person or committee who invited you to minister. In addition, having a thorough understanding of protocol for the specific church or denomination you will be ministering to helps bridge gaps and gives honor where it is due. Romans 13:6-7 says:

> For this cause pay ye tribute also: for they are God's ministers, attending continually upon this very thing. Render therefore to all their dues: tribute to whom tribute is due; custom to whom custom; fear to whom fear; honour to whom honour.

You can also use your opening greetings and acknowledgements to lead into your message.

Discuss what God is doing in your life (don't brag; give God the glory), or give a brief testimony. Then, proceed with your message.

2. State Your Subject

Using our sample subject from Chapter 1, at this point, tell your listeners you will be speaking on the topic, "Warriors for God."

3. Give Your Scripture Reference Text

Here you'll read your text scripture aloud or ask someone to read it for you. At this point, I sometimes like to present my scripture reference text from different versions of the Bible, such as the King James Version (KJV), the Amplified Bible or the New International Version (NIV), if I feel a particular translation of scripture will help me build a strong foundation for understanding my message.

4. Explain the Text

At this point, your main goal is to build a strong foundation for your message to stand upon. So, you'll want to define key words in the text to help your listeners better understand how the text relates to your subject. Use this time to present the Hebrew or Greek meanings of specific key words that you've found to support your subject, as discussed in Chapter 1. Now, on to Step 5.

5. Discuss Your Biblical Examples

Now that you've built a strong foundation for your message, your next goal is to build the support beams for the structure of your sermon. At this time, use your biblical examples you've selected to support your subject. Submit to the Spirit's leading. You will find that each time you deliver a message, the Spirit will move through you to select points of interest from your biblical examples that your listeners will be able to relate to. Don't try to relay absolutely everything you've studied or prepared. Instead, let the Spirit flow through you to minister to your listeners based on what they need. The Spirit knows what your listeners need—just follow Him!

Preparation, however, is vital because throughout your delivery, the Spirit will use your level of understanding to bring forth what you've implanted in your spirit. John 14:26 says, "But the Comforter, which is the Holy Ghost, whom the Father will send in my name, he shall teach you all things, and bring all things to your remembrance, whatsoever I have said unto you."

One biblical example we chose in Chapter 1 was Samson's battle with the Philistines. So at this point, you would want to discuss Samson's strong skills as a warrior and how he defeated many Philistines when the Spirit of God came upon him. You could say that Samson was a warrior appointed by God to stand against Israel's enemies, but he couldn't overcome them unless the Spirit was upon him. Then drive the point home by letting the hearers know they can't defeat their enemies unless they are moved by the Spirit, and they must avoid warring in the flesh.

We can then move on to the second biblical example we chose, which was David's battle with Goliath. Here we could discuss that despite David's small stature, he still defeated the giant because God was fighting on his side. To drive the point home, let your hearers know that no matter how big the obstacles in their lives are, they can overcome them by depending on God's power within them. Use other support scriptures, such as Romans 8:37, to drive the point home further: "Nay, in all these things we are more than conquerors through him that loved us." Let's move right along to Step 6.

6. Bring It Up to Date

Now, use everyday events that relate to your subject to bring your topic up to date. Remember in Chapter 1, we chose the warriors of Desert Storm for our sample message. Mention how these brave fighters increasingly used more advanced weapons because their enemy was also continually upgrading its weaponry. You can add that as warriors for God, we must continually use more advanced weapons because our war with the kingdom of darkness has increased, and we must stand ready to fight the enemy with all the spiritual weapons we as believers have available.

As stated in Chapter 1, here you can also use your own personal experiences of standing as a "Warrior for God." If you do this, however, use extreme caution and wisdom regarding exactly what to reveal. If your experience involves other people, refrain from giving names of individuals, places, ministries or businesses. Remember, your job as a messenger for God is to build one another up, not tear one another down. The intimate details of your experiences are not necessary to be effective when driving your points home. They mainly stand to help the hearers relate to your overall subject. Nor should your personal experiences be used to glorify yourself; bring glory to God instead. Let us conclude our message in Step 7.

7. Recap Your Points and Conclude the Message

You want the Word to leave a positive impression on your listeners' hearts and minds.

As you conclude your message, leave your listeners in a frame of mind for rejoicing, or more importantly, moving toward change or repentance. For our chosen subject, "Warriors for God," you can conclude by letting your listeners know that they are more than conquerors through Christ Jesus, as stated in Romans 8:37, and through Him we have all power over the enemy, as relayed in Luke 10:19.

Also, when concluding your message remember: If the Holy Spirit is finished, you should be finished. Many messengers err when they get off of God's focus for that particular hour. That's why being led by the Spirit is so crucial. You don't have to say everything you've studied or have written in your notes. Also, set time limits for your delivery. If your message is too long, you may lose your listeners' attention and miss your target goal, which is to edify.

8. End With a Prayer

This prayer should be related to the message just ministered. Using our subject, "Warriors for God," as an example, we could pray that each listener becomes a warrior for God and stands in victory over Satan.

This concludes our lesson, but let me emphasize again that when you deliver your message, make sure you use scriptures to back up your subject. Also, pray that God allows you to deliver your message with anointing and power because that is what will ultimately change lives and destroy the yokes of darkness. 2 Corinthians 3:6 says, *"The letter killeth but the spirit giveth life."*

 **Chapter 3** | # FASTING AND PRAYER: KEYS TO MINISTRY

Now that we've discussed the mechanics of preparing and delivering a message, let's deal with heart and spirit preparation, which should always be done before any words are ever written down. Fasting and prayer are two of the most important keys to ministering effectively because they condition your spirit and place you in the presence or mind of God; making you an effective conduit for God's power and presence. This, in turn, causes you to minister or speak as God would speak to bring life into any situation.

According to Psalms 35:13, fasting and prayer humble you and cause you to subject your will to God's. They open your spirit and make you more God-conscious. Fasting and prayer also cleanse you. And when you are cleansed, you become a vessel that releases the yoke-destroying anointing and power of God upon the earth.

The Word of God constantly mentions fasting and prayer and gives several examples of men and women who fasted and prayed and got results. Refer to Nehemiah 1:4, Acts 13:1-3 and Acts 14:23 for examples. Fasting and prayer also launched Jesus' ministry, according to Matthew 4:2, which in and of itself should indicate how vital these keys to effective ministry are. Since fasting and prayer are so important, let's see exactly what they are all about.

Fasting

Webster's definition of fasting reads: *Abstaining from food; To deny one's self certain foods as a form of religious discipline.* Seems like a simple definition, doesn't it? Unfortunately, much controversy exists in the church about what constitutes a true fast. Some say you are not truly fasting unless you are only drinking water and totally abstaining from all forms of food. Others say that you can fast by abstaining from certain types of foods and drinking juice with water.

Even though I agree that a true fast is totally abstaining from food, I also feel that you can fast by abstaining from certain foods, which is illustrated by Daniel 1:8-16. Types of fasting include:

- **A Total Fast:** Abstaining from all forms of food and only drinking water.

- **A Juice Fast:** Abstaining from all forms of food except juices.

- **A Vegetable and Fruit Fast:** Eating only salads, fresh vegetables and fruit.

Note: Please drink water with each fast to flush your system. Also see Figure-1 (page 45) for "The Complete Fast," which is a fast that God gave to me that incorporates all of these fasts. Try it and allow God to bring results in your life and ministry. Let God lead you to the fast that's right for you.

The bottom line is that God will honor any sacrifice you give Him. But keep in mind the greater the sacrifice, the greater the reward. Luke 12:48 says that to whom much is given much is required. He also honors you when you abstain from other forms of pleasure, such as watching television, in favor of studying God's Word for a week and listening to what He tells you. God will definitely honor this sacrifice and reward accordingly.

Prayer

Before a minister or leader can be an effective spokesperson for God, he or she must first know God. This is where the power of prayer comes in. Prayer is communication between God and man. It's not a monologue, which involves only one person speaking; it's a dialog that involves two parties speaking to one another. Prayer allows man to know God in His fullness.

The best way to get to know someone is by communicating and spending time with that person. Eventually, you will come to know that person fully. But if you never spend time or communicate with someone, you will never get to know that person. Since we as fallen humans don't completely know God, we need to pray to the Father and be reconciled to Him. That is the only way we will ever know Him. If we do not know Him, we certainly can't fully speak in His stead. Colossians 4:2-4 (NIV) says:

> Devote yourselves to prayer, being watchful and thankful. And pray for us, too, that God may open a door for our message, so that we may proclaim the mystery of Christ, for which I am in chains. Pray that I may proclaim it clearly, as I should.

In addition, 2 Corinthians 5:20 (NIV), proclaims that we are ambassadors for Christ: "We are therefore Christ's ambassadors, as though God were making his appeal through us. We implore you on Christ's behalf: Be reconciled to God." Webster's definition of an ambassador reads: "An official representative of the highest rank, accredited by one government to another." As ambassadors for Christ, we are sent to represent the Kingdom, or the government of God, to the governments of this world, be they spiritual or natural.

Regularly communicating with God through prayer allows us to think how He thinks and move how He moves. This permits us to function in our ministries as He would, which should be our main purpose as ministers and leaders. We must be able to say, "When you see me, you see the Father because we are one." Let's look at John 17:20-23, the prayer Jesus prayed concerning us:

> Neither pray I for these alone, but for them also which shall believe on me through their word; That they all may be one; as thou, Father, art in me, and I in thee, that they also may be one in us: that the world may

believe that thou hast sent me. And the glory which thou gavest me I have given them; that they may be one, even as we are one: I in them, and thou in me, that they may be made perfect in one; and that the world may know that thou hast sent me, and hast loved them, as thou hast loved me.

We must also pray this way so that we can be one with the Father and speak as the oracles of God. Many of us find it hard to pray because we don't know how. There are many ways to approach God's throne. Here's a simple format to get you started until you are able to discern the method that's comfortable for you.

1. Ask For Forgiveness of Sins

Doing this first will allow you to come before God's throne pure and without hindrances.

Psalms 66:18 says that "If I regard iniquity in my heart, the Lord will not hear me." Coming before God with a clean slate opens His heart to hear your prayers.

2. Give Thanks and Praise to God

This allows you to really get God's attention and welcome His presence. Psalms 22:3 says that God inhabits the praises of His people. His power is released through praise.

3. Pray For Your Leaders

Offer a prayer of guidance for those who lead. This list includes overseers, pastors, teachers, as well as U.S. and world leaders. Hebrews 13:7 says, "Remember them which have the rule over you, who have spoken unto you the word of God: whose faith follow, considering the end of their conversation."

4. Pray For Others

This is where you may have to stand in the gap or intercede for someone, so make sure you really let the Spirit lead. James 5:16 says, "Confess your faults one to another, and pray one for another, that ye may be healed. The effectual fervent prayer of a righteous man availeth much."

5. Pray For Yourself

Here again, let the Spirit lead; you can't go wrong doing so. This is a good opportunity to confess your faults and shortcomings and ask for God's help and deliverance. Pray for God's guidance so that you will forever stay in His perfect will. David, one of the greatest ministers of the Old Testament, practiced this principle oh so well. Let's look at Psalms 32:5-7:

> I acknowledged my sin unto thee, and mine iniquity have I not hid. I said, I will confess my transgressions unto the LORD; and thou forgavest the iniquity of my sin. Selah. For this shall every one that is godly pray unto thee in a time when thou mayest be found: surely in the floods of great waters they shall not come nigh unto him. Thou art my hiding place; thou shalt preserve me from trouble; thou shalt compass me about with songs of deliverance. Selah.

6. Give God Thanks

Thank God for hearing and answering your prayers, as demonstrated by Philippians 4:6. Giving God thanks at this point is actually a step of faith because it shows that you believe God has heard your prayers and will answer accordingly.

7. Listen

At this point, listen to see if God will speak to your spirit concerning anything you have just prayed about. As mentioned before, prayer is a dialogue, not a monologue. Waiting quietly after you have prayed gives God, through the Holy Spirit, an opportunity to speak to you concerning His will for you.

I encourage you to follow this format if you don't already have an effective way to pray. I would also like to add: pray in the Spirit (in tongues) as often as you can, because this strengthens your spiritual man. Jude 1:20 declares, "But ye, beloved, building up yourselves on your most holy faith, praying in the Holy Spirit."

In addition, Romans 8:26-27 states:

> Likewise the Spirit also helpeth our infirmities: for we know not what we should

pray for as we ought: but the Spirit itself maketh intercession for us with groanings which cannot be uttered. And he that searcheth the hearts knoweth what is the mind of the Spirit, because he maketh intercession for the saints according to the will of God.

And finally, Matthew 17:19-21 provides another important reason to fast and pray—to cure unbelief! In this passage, Jesus tells his disciples that because of their unbelief they couldn't cast out the devil: "Howbeit this kind goeth not out but by prayer and fasting."

Now that we have established the importance of fasting and praying, I ask that you put what you have learned into practice so that God will open doors to new levels of ministry for you.

Different Types of Prayer

Ephesians 6:18 says to pray always with all prayer and supplication in the Spirit. Below is a short list of different types of prayer.

- Prayer of Supplication
  1 Kings 8:37-40, Luke 11:9-13

- Prayer of Faith
  Matthew 9:18-26, Luke 7:1-10

- Prayer of Praise & Thanksgiving
  Psalm 100, I Thessalonians 5:16-19

- Prayer of Agreement
  Matthew 18:19-20

- Prayer of Intercession
  Genesis 18:22-33, Acts 12:1-18

FIGURE-1 - THE COMPLETE FAST

Sunday	Monday	Tuesday	Wednesday	Thursday	Friday	Saturday
1	2	3	4	5	6	7
1st Week of Fasting — No beef or pork - ONLY poultry, fish, vegetables, fruits, juice, water							
8	9	10	11	12	13	14
2nd Week of Fasting — No beef, pork, poultry - ONLY fish, vegetables, fruits, juice, water							
15	16	17	18	19	20	21
3rd Week of Fasting — No beef, pork, poultry, fish - ONLY vegetables, fruits, juice, water							
22	23	24	25	26	27	28
4th Week of Fasting — No beef, pork, poultry, fish, vegetables - ONLY fruits, juice, water							
29	30	31	1 New Month	2	3	4
5th Week of Fasting — No beef, pork, poultry, fish, vegetables, fruits - ONLY juice, water							
5	6	7	8	9	10	11
6th Week of Fasting — No beef, pork, poultry, fish, vegetables, fruits, juice, - ONLY water							

*Refrain from eating sweets, fried foods, bread, grains and drinking coffee, soft drinks, etc.

KEYS TO REMEMBER WHEN FASTING

- Pray. Listen for God's voice. Follow it.
- Drink plenty of water during your fast.
- Fast according to Matthew 6:16-18.
- Study and meditate upon Isaiah 58.
- Be conscious of what you expose yourself to while fasting.
- Break your fast gradually, starting with juice and light foods.
- Consult a doctor before going on an extended fast, especially if health is an issue for you.
- Be led by the Spirit on how long to fast.
- Read *God's Chosen Fast, A Spiritual and Practical Guide to Fasting*, Arthur Wallis, (Christian Literature Crusade, 1997).

 *Chapter* | How to Study God's Word

In this lesson we will cover the significance of studying God's Word and discuss specific steps to accomplish this goal. First of all, let us look at the word "study". Webster's dictionary defines it as, "The application of the mind to books to gain knowledge." 2 Timothy 2:15 instructs us to "Study to show thyself approved unto God, a workman that needeth not to be ashamed, rightly dividing the word of truth."

So, why is God telling us to study or apply our minds to His Word? The answer to that question is found in 2 Timothy 2:16-18:

> But shun profane and vain babblings: for they will increase unto more ungodliness. And their word will eat as doth a canker: of whom is Hymenaeus and Philetus; Who concerning the truth have erred, saying that the resurrection is past already; and overthrow the faith of some.

Here, Paul is telling us that through the negligence of two ministers, Hymenaeus and Philetus, many were misled by the words they brought forth because they did not study God's Word. And because they neglected to study, their messages were considered "profane and vain babblings." As ministers, we should exercise extreme caution when we speak. We do not want any of our messages to be perceived as "profane and vain babblings." We could really cause injury to a soul who is relying on every word we say. Surely that soul will be required at your hand.

Now that we know why it's important to study God's Word, let's examine how we should engage in accomplishing this mission. Following are four key steps to effective Bible study.

1. Choose a Subject and Research it Thoroughly

If you are particularly interested in the subject of "The Holy Ghost," for example, prepare to do extensive research on this topic. First, study all the scriptures on the Holy Ghost using the Bible and a good concordance. Compare the scriptures to see if you can achieve a complete understanding.

In addition, reading as many books as you can on your chosen subject helps you see another person's perspective. Since we are all on different spiritual levels, it's always good to see how God speaks to other individuals on particular subjects of interest.

2. Attend Bible Studies, Church Services, Conferences and Seminars

Here is where you can definitely increase your knowledge concerning God's Word. Make sure you take along paper and a pencil to keep notes. You never know when a point may be explained particularly well or divine revelation will come to you. As ministers or leaders, we must always maintain a humble, teachable spirit; for this is how we grow stronger in our ministry.

3. Expose Yourself to God's Word Constantly

The more you expose yourself to God's Word, the more familiar you will be with it, and the least likely you will be to err concerning the truth. So, listen to Christian radio and television; just make sure you're listening to biblically sound sources.

If you are riding in your car, play an audio recording of your favorite minister, or tune your radio to a Christian station. If you're at home, tune your television to a Christian channel for spiritual inspiration. Playing a teaching or preaching message while you're sleeping is another good way to take in God's Word. I firmly believe that while you are sleeping, your subconscious mind (spirit) takes in all that is heard, and will recall it when needed, as illustrated in John 14:26.

4. Study Regularly and Seek God for Understanding

Choose a special time each day when you can sit quietly to study God's Word and meditate on His truth. Studying and meditating on God's Word opens doors to greater revelation. For in times of meditation, your mind is in a position to hear what God wants to say to you, as stated in 1 Timothy 4:13-16.

Meditation involves taking a particular word, scripture or truth and listening quietly for the voice of God. As you continue listening, God reveals Himself to you through His Word, causing the eyes of your understanding to be enlightened, as indicated in Ephesians 1:17-18. Meditation is taking studying to a higher level, thus bringing greater results.

Let me add one final thought. Don't wait until you get an engagement to minister and then do an intense study the night before you speak. The results will be similar to those received after you've crammed the night before an exam. Studying God's Word should be ongoing in the life of a minister. So don't let God down, study to show thyself approved, a workman that needeth not to be ashamed, rightly dividing the Word of truth.

Chapter  WISDOM IN MINISTRY

This chapter is about the value of applying wisdom in ministry. Proverbs 4:5, 7 says: *"Get wisdom, get understanding: forget it not; neither decline from the words of my mouth. Wisdom is the principal thing; therefore get wisdom: and with all thy getting get understanding."* In this verse, the word principal means: that which is first and foremost in importance. As ministers and leaders, wisdom is like what is said of the American Express Card—*don't leave home without it.*

Wisdom is the understanding of what is true. It's the ability to say and do the right thing at the right time and place. It's showing good judgment.

God often entrusts ministers and leaders with various forms of knowledge. Whether it be the mysteries of the Kingdom, or the intimate details of someone's life, we must know how to handle any situation with wisdom; because we will constantly be placed in positions of authority and power due to the knowledge that we have received from God. And the more God reveals, the more power we possess. Remember the old saying: *Knowledge is power*. The more power we receive, the more we are placed in circumstances where we affect situations, people and outcomes.

In any given situation, your use of wisdom may be the determining factor in whether you: help a person to succeed or fail, a church to grow or die, a business to prosper or become bankrupt, and most importantly, whether a soul is lost or saved. Proverbs 11:30 says, *"He that winneth souls is wise."*

Make sure, however, you're not pressured into using your own judgment or wisdom in a situation. 1 Corinthians 3:18-19 says: "Let no man deceive himself. If any man among you seemeth to be wise in this world, let him become a fool, that he may be wise. For the wisdom of this world is foolishness with God...." Man's wisdom and God's wisdom are not the same. In some cases, the use of human reasoning could prove to be fatal; therefore, you must use Godly wisdom in ministry just as Jesus did. Let's look at John 8:1-11 for an example of how Jesus exercised Godly wisdom.

The scene opens with the scribes and Pharisees bringing to Jesus a woman caught in adultery. They asked Jesus how she should be punished for her deeds. Jesus, knowing their motives, displayed great wisdom. Not only was his life at stake, but so was hers. His reply was, "He that is without sin cast the first stone." One by one, all of the woman's accusers walked away.

Just think for one moment what would have happened if Jesus had used His human reasoning and not the wisdom from His Father (for he was 100 percent man and 100 percent God). The outcome could have been devastating had he not spoken in His Father's wisdom. Both He and the woman could have been stoned to death. We ourselves could have been left without a Savior if God's plan had been altered.

Now can you see how important it is to use wisdom? So, how do you obtain Godly wisdom? Simple! Go to the source according to James 1:5: "If any of you lack wisdom, let him ask of God, that giveth to all men liberally, and upbraideth not; and it shall be given him."

A perfect example of this promise being fulfilled is in 1 Kings 3, which is the account of

King Solomon asking God for wisdom and the manifestation thereof. As you read the passage, remember that Romans 2:11 says that God is no respecter of persons. If God granted Solomon the wisdom he needed, He most certainly can do the same for you.

So, as you endeavor in ministry, remember to use extreme caution by operating in wisdom. The situation or life you save may very well be your own. And keep in mind 1 Corinthians 2:16 and Matthew 10:16, which urge us to have the mind of Christ and walk in wisdom.

Wisdom Keys For Ministry

- Seek God diligently with fasting and prayer before you go forth to minister. (Mark 9:24-29)

- Stay sober and vigilant when entering old and new territory. (1 Peter 5:8-9, Titus 1:9-2:6)

- Move only when the Spirit leads. Learn to flow in the Spirit. (John 16:13, Romans 8:14)

- Go forth with a ministry partner who can cover you spiritually on the ministry field. (Mark 6:7)

- Seek wise counsel and spiritual mentors who know the way. (Proverbs 24:6)

- Abide in your calling. Minister according to your level of grace and faith. (Romans 12:6)

 *Chapter* | THE FIVE-FOLD MINISTRY

As a final chapter in our study of preparing for ministry, we will discuss the components of what is known as "The Five-Fold Ministry." The Five-Fold Ministry consists of the gifts of the following five groups of people:

1. **Apostles**   4. **Pastors**
2. **Prophets**   5. **Teachers**
3. **Evangelists**

The Five-Fold Ministry is a significant part of the Body of Christ and is given expressly for the perfecting or maturing of the church. Let's look at Ephesians 4:11-13:

> And he gave some, apostles; and some, prophets; and some, evangelists; and

some, pastors and teachers; For the perfecting of the saints, for the work of the ministry, for the edifying of the body of Christ: Till we all come in the unity of the faith, and of the knowledge of the Son of God, unto a perfect man, unto the measure of the stature of the fulness of Christ.

God gave these ministries to the church as earthly representations of His Divine Self. Each ministry represents the multifaceted God we serve. When Jesus walked upon this earth, He was a manifestation of all the ministries wrapped into one. He was the fullness of God bodily according to Colossians 1:19 and 2:9. To get a clearer picture, let's define and give an example for each of these five facets of ministry:

1. Apostles

Apostles are sent with the full authority of God to establish and build up the church. They are skilled laborers in foundational teaching and works. Their job is to lay the groundwork for a ministry. Apostles are those sent as pioneers and are capable of functioning in every ministry if need be. A good example of an apostle is Paul, according to Galatians 1:1.

2. Prophets

Prophets are watchmen of God and deal closely with the mind of God. By the Spirit, prophets know the thoughts and plans of God and the plans of others. They receive supernatural revelations of the past, present and future. Oftentimes, prophets keep to themselves and devote much time to consecration and serving God. Prophets also frequently deal in the realm of the Spirit. There are different administrations of this ministry, and each has a specific function in the Body of Christ. For a more in-depth study of the ministry of a prohet,

I suggest you read *The Seer*, by James Goll, published by Destiny Image.

Keep in mind, however, that just because someone possesses the gift of prophecy that does not mean that he or she stands in the office of a prophet. The difference between the two lies in the operation in conjunction with the Spirit. A person who has the gift of prophecy usually brings forth a message after the rendering of tongues according to 1 Corinthians 14:27-33. On the other hand, a prophet simply says, "Thus said the Lord," eliminating the middleman. A prophet deals directly with the mind of God, receiving the message firsthand, while the person with the gift goes through channels. A person with the gift, therefore, may only have the spirit of the prophet and not the ministry. A good example of a prophet is Elijah in 1 Kings 17.

3. Evangelists

Evangelists are those sent to restore, refresh, root up, tear down and build up. They are constantly on the move and become easily frustrated in spirit when they are not in action. Evangelists can sometimes be the best remedy for a troubled church because they can say things the pastor can't normally say. By the anointing and power of the Holy Spirit, they straighten out situations and set God's house in order. They also aid in periods of transition with words of counsel and encouragement. Philip *(biblical spelling of his name)* is our example of an evangelist found in Acts 21:8.

4. Pastors

Pastors are shepherds who have been appointed by God to be watchmen and guides over a specific group of people. Pastors stand as a covering and hedge for those in their care. Unlike evangelists, pastors are usually stationary. They are usually full of much patience and love and play great roles in nurturing and developing a church because they strive to bring out the best in all. Pastors are men and women after God's own heart, as indicated in Jeremiah 3:15. A good example of a pastor is Timothy in 1 and 2 Timothy.

5. Teachers

Teachers are those able to expound on the Word of God, bringing out points that the reader wouldn't normally see. Teachers are able to simplify the Word so all who hear it can understand. They tend to give much time to study and are scholars of God's laws. In the church, they help dispel misconceptions; allowing the Body to maintain a clear vision. Jesus was one of the greatest teachers that ever lived, as seen in John 3:2.

In closing, let me say that it's entirely possible for one person to operate in more than one ministry. Many today are evangelists as well as pastors. Many pastors are also avid teachers. Jesus most certainly operated in all of these ministries.

In addition, not everyone operates in these ministry gifts. If everyone did, the Body would be one-sided and deformed, as indicated by 1 Corinthians 12:4-6, 28-29. These passages speak of the diversity among the different gifts of administration, operation, helps, government and tongues.

So, seek the Lord to find your place in ministry. Then place yourself, so the body can function as it should and go on to perfection.

About the Author

Tarsha is a dynamic, God-appointed Woman of Destiny who flows under a strong prophetic anointing. God has called Tarsha to teach His people who He is and their true identity in Him. With this mandate she humbly serves as a licensed minister, a compelling Bible teacher, inspirational speaker, certified Christian life coach, spiritual midwife, and ministry and business consultant.

Since childhood Tarsha has possessed a love for the truth and the meat of God's Word. It is through this love that God has birthed life-altering prophetic teachings that are reaching people from all walks of life around the world. Tarsha is most known for the powerful teaching series, *"The Woman in the Mirror"*, which has imparted life to those who desire to walk in their true identity in Christ. Her unique, illustrated teaching style has allowed many to "see" and "understand" what the Father is saying with complete clarity, practical application, and unprecedented spiritual breakthrough!

Tarsha is a published author. Her book titles include: *Called and Chosen: A Study Guide to Ministry*, *Help! I've Been Called By God: Easy Steps to Preparing and Delivering a Message*, and *5 Qualities of a Woman of Destiny*. God's vision for her life also includes helping other ministers publish their writings so she has launched Dominionhouse Publishing & Design, a publishing and graphic design firm dedicated to publishing the gospel with divine ingenuity and creative excellence. Tarsha is also the Executive Director of Revealed International Women's Empowerment Network, Inc., an organization dedicated to helping women unveil their God-given identity, potential, purpose, & destiny.

Tarsha believes there is nothing we can't do if we learn to tap into the divine mind of God and walk in who we really are in Him. She resides in the Orlando area with her husband of 21 years and their two children.

Contact the Author

Please email or write the author with any comments you may have. You are also welcome to contact her for bookings. As the Holy Spirit leads, Tarsha is available for book club presentations, signings, or speaking engagements for your church or organization (women's ministries, women's clubs, conferences, workshops, retreats, and seminars). Contact her at:

tarsha@revealedinternational.com
www.revealedinternational.com
P.O. Box 681938
Orlando, Florida 32868
407.880.5790

BE INSPIRED!

Available now from DOMINIONHOUSE
Great for individual or group study

Woman of Destiny, arise! Your time has come! The Word of the Lord has been spoken! Your day is at hand, but do you have what it takes?

5 Qualities of a Woman of Destiny was written with you in mind. As a Woman of Destiny you must possess certain qualities to succeed in God's plan and purpose for your life. This book will help you tap into hidden qualities yet to be revealed in you!

Order your copy today! Available at:
**www.revealedinternational.com
amazon.com and other fine book retailers
Just ask for the book**

Do *YOU* know *YOUR LIFE PURPOSE...*
Why *YOU* were created and what is *YOUR DIVINE DESIGN?*
We can HELP YOU...

REVEALED

REVEALED INTERNATIONAL | WOMEN'S EMPOWERMENT NETWORK, INC.

Helping women
unveil their
God-given identity,
potential, purpose,
& destiny.

INTERNATIONAL

Our passion is to empower women to embrace divine fulfillment through spiritual and personal growth and development.

YOUR LINK TO
SUCCESS & FULFILLMENT
Make the Connection!

WWW.REVEALEDINTERNATIONAL.COM

The Mission of DOMINIONHOUSE Publishing & Design

**The Lord gave the word: great was the company of those that published it.
(Psalms 68:11)**

DOMINIONHOUSE Publishing & Design is dedicated to providing an outlet for those who have been "given a word." It is with this dedication to the Gospel that we offer quality custom publishing products and services, catered exclusively for the Body of Christ. It is our commitment to work cooperatively with you, the author, to bring the Gospel to the world, that we may experience DOMINION in all levels of living!

For more information visit:
www.mydominionhouse.com

Practice Message

Use the outline provided below to prepare a message/sermon

I. Message/Sermon Subject

    A. _____

    _____

II. Scripture Reference Text(s)

    A. _____

    B. _____

III. Two Biblical Examples to Support My Subject

    A. _____

    B. _____

IV. Up-to-Date Examples to Support My Subject

    A. _____

    B. _____

    C. _____

V. Message/Sermon Conclusion

   A. Reinforce/reiterate my points

   _____

   _____

   _____

   _____

   _____

   _____

   _____

   _____

   B. Closing Statements/Prayer

   _____

   _____

   _____

   _____

   _____

   _____

   _____

   _____

   _____

   _____

Practice Message

Use the outline provided below to prepare a message/sermon

I. Message/Sermon Subject

   A. _____

   _____

II. Scripture Reference Text(s)

   A. _____

   B. _____

III. Two Biblical Examples to Support My Subject

   A. _____

   B. _____

IV. Up-to-Date Examples to Support My Subject

   A. _____

   B. _____

   C. _____

V. Message/Sermon Conclusion

　　A. Reinforce/reiterate my points

　　———————————————————

　　———————————————————

　　———————————————————

　　———————————————————

　　———————————————————

　　———————————————————

　　———————————————————

　　———————————————————

　　B. Closing Statements/Prayer

　　———————————————————

　　———————————————————

　　———————————————————

　　———————————————————

　　———————————————————

　　———————————————————

　　———————————————————

　　———————————————————

　　———————————————————

Practice Message

Use the outline provided below to prepare a message/sermon

I. Message/Sermon Subject

  A. _____

  _____

II. Scripture Reference Text(s)

  A. _____

  B. _____

III. Two Biblical Examples to Support My Subject

  A. _____

  B. _____

IV. Up-to-Date Examples to Support My Subject

  A. _____

  B. _____

  C. _____

V. Message/Sermon Conclusion

    A. Reinforce/reiterate my points

    B. Closing Statements/Prayer

Note Page

Note Page

Note Page

www.ingramcontent.com/pod-product-compliance
Lightning Source LLC
Chambersburg PA
CBHW071331040426
42444CB00009B/2129